CONTENTS

HOW DO WE USE WATER?

Water keeps us and all plants and animals alive. Our bodies will not work without it. We get water from our food and drink.

Water also keeps us clean. In a bath or under a shower, water washes away dirt and grease from our skin. We also use water to wash our dishes, clothes, homes, cars, and streets.

Clean water flows out of faucets in our kitchens and bathrooms. To clean dishes, we add detergent to the water. Detergent removes fats and oils from the food, making it come off the plate easier.

WATER

BRENDA WILLIAMS

RAINTREE
STECK-VAUGHN
PUBLISHERS
A Steck-Vaughn Company

Austin, Texas

ENVIRONMENT STARTS HERE

TITLES IN THE SERIES
Food · Recycling · Transportation · Water

Published by Raintree Steck-Vaughn Publishers,
an imprint of Steck-Vaughn Company

Library of Congress Cataloging-in-Publication Data
Williams, Brenda.
Water / Brenda Williams.
    p.   cm.—(Environment starts here)
    Includes bibliographical references and index.
    Summary: Discusses where water is found, where it goes, and how we use it.
    ISBN 0-8172-5350-5
    1. Water—Juvenile literature.
    [1. Water.]
    I. Title. II. Series.
    GB662.3.W545 1999
    551.48—dc21   98-4589

Printed in Italy. Bound in the United States.
1 2 3 4 5 6 7 8 9 0 03 02 01 00 99
Picture Acknowledgments
Pages 1, 4: Angela Hampton Family Life Pictures. 5: Wayland Picture Library. 6: Zefa Photo Library. 8: Tony Stone Images/David Woodfall. 9: Tony Stone Images/Laurence Dutton. 10-11: Eye Ubiquitous/K. Wilton. 12: Eye Ubiquitous/John Dakers. 13: Tony Stone Images/David Woodfall. 14: Eye Ubiquitous/J. B. Pickering. 15: Eye Ubiquitous/L. Fordyce. 16: Zefa Photo Library/Norman. 18: Angela Hampton Family Life Pictures. 20: Eye Ubiquitous/C. M. Leask. 20-21: Zefa Photo Library/Stockmarket. 22: Angela Hampton Family Life Pictures. 24: Eye Ubiquitous/G. Daniels. 26: Frank Lane Picture Agency/David Hosking. 26-27: Tony Stone Images/Vince Streano. 28: Angela Hampton Family Life Pictures. 29: Tony Stone Images/Patrick Cocklin. Cover: Zefa Photo Library/Stockmarket.
Illustrated by Rudi Vizi

The photo on page 1 shows children splashing in water at the seaside.

We use water to clean our teeth and to rinse the toothpaste from our mouths.

Flowing Around the House

Clean water flows to our homes from pipes under the street. Pipes inside our homes carry the water to and from the kitchen, bathroom, and boiler.

We each use about 30 bucketfuls of clean water a day. A toilet flush uses about 2 bucketfuls and a bath about 12 bucketfuls. The rest is water we use for drinking, cooking, or washing dishes.

A plumber attaches a radiator to a central heating pipe. Hot water flowing through radiators heats air in rooms in some houses.

Saving Water

Next time you take a bath, make a note of how far up the water comes. (Measure the height with a ruler.) Then, when you have a shower, leave the plug in and measure the height of water when you are done. Which uses the most water: a bath or a shower?

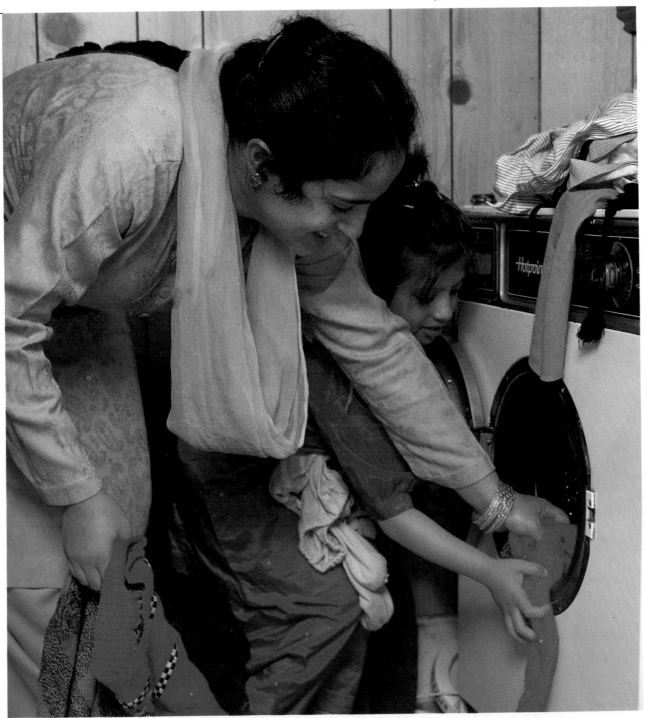

Water helps us all around the house. This girl and her mother are unloading their washing machine which uses water piped into the house.

WHERE DOES THE WATER GO?

Used, dirty water with soapsuds or bits of waste food runs down a drain. From there it flows down a waste pipe.

Water from a toilet carries away our body wastes. It flows down the waste pipe, too.

Dirty water flows from the waste pipe into a drain under the street. This runs into a bigger pipe called a sewer.

Floodwater pours out of a sewer cover. When rainwater drains into sewers already full with water from houses, the sewers overflow.

Water flowing down
a drain swirls around
in a spiral.

Down to the River

The main sewers are as big as railroad tunnels. Waste water flows along them to a sewage plant. There the dirty water is cleaned of all harmful germs.

At the sewage plant, muddy waste called sludge is taken away and spread on unused land. Cleaned water then flows out into rivers and canals.

At a sewage plant, waste water from houses, schools, offices, and factories trickles through filter beds that remove grit and harmful materials from the water.

Gas outlet pipe

Septic tank

Surface of ground

Cleaned water

Dirty water from house

Sludge

Some homes have septic tanks to treat waste water. Bacteria in the tanks turn dirt and grease into a sludge. Cleaned water seeps out along pipes into the soil. Some of the sludge turns into a gas that escapes into the air. The rest is pumped out of the tank.

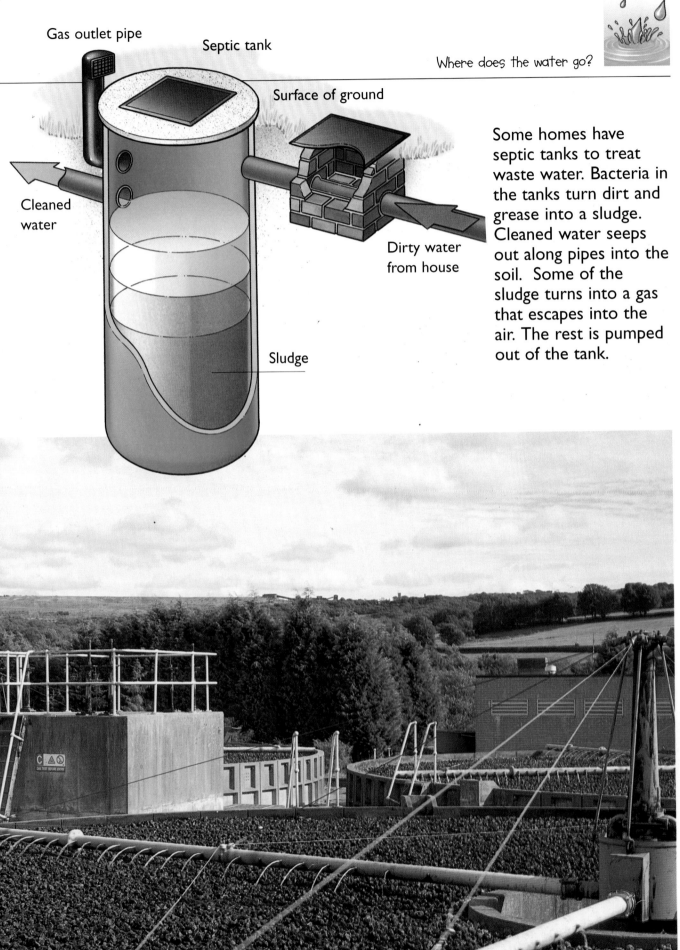

Rivers flow into the sea. They take with them water from sewage works and any factory waste and garbage thrown in rivers.

If too much waste material is dumped in the sea, it can poison, or pollute, the water. This may kill creatures living in the sea.

Seawater is too salty to drink. Here on the coast of Thailand salt for cooking is being collected from seawater.

Uncleaned sewage is sometimes pumped along huge outlet pipes like this one straight into the sea.

Steam rises into the air from huge smokestacks at a power plant. Steam is made when water becomes very hot.

Up into the Clouds

As the sun warms the sea, some of its water turns into a vapor, or gas. This rises into the sky. High up, the vapor cools into water droplets that form clouds.

Smoke and fumes from fires and factories also rise into the air. They mix with the clouds. Rain from these clouds may be so poisonous that it kills fish and plants.

Rain pours from thick gray clouds that hang low in the sky.

To protect ourselves
from the rain, we use
umbrellas or wear
raincoats. Here,
sunlight has lit falling
raindrops, which makes
them easy to see.

Falling as Rain

Clouds are made of millions of water droplets. Tiny water droplets bump into each other and join to make bigger, heavier droplets. Eventually, the droplets become so heavy they fall out of the clouds as rain.

Rain often falls on high ground, then trickles into rivers. Rivers flow across the land and finally empty into the sea.

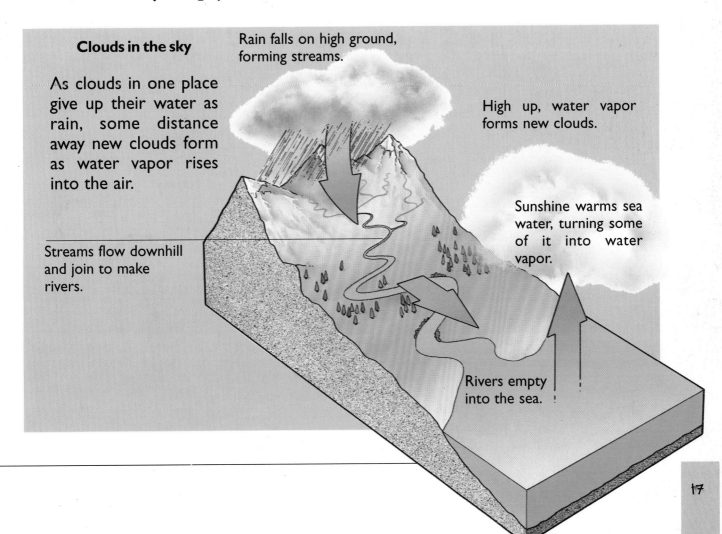

Clouds in the sky

As clouds in one place give up their water as rain, some distance away new clouds form as water vapor rises into the air.

Streams flow downhill and join to make rivers.

Rain falls on high ground, forming streams.

High up, water vapor forms new clouds.

Sunshine warms sea water, turning some of it into water vapor.

Rivers empty into the sea.

WATER ON THE GROUND

Next time it rains, watch where the water goes. It runs down drains in the road. It runs off roofs and soaks into the soil.

If rainwater cannot run away, it makes a puddle. Pools, ponds, and lakes are like big puddles. They are hollows in the ground that do not empty all their water.

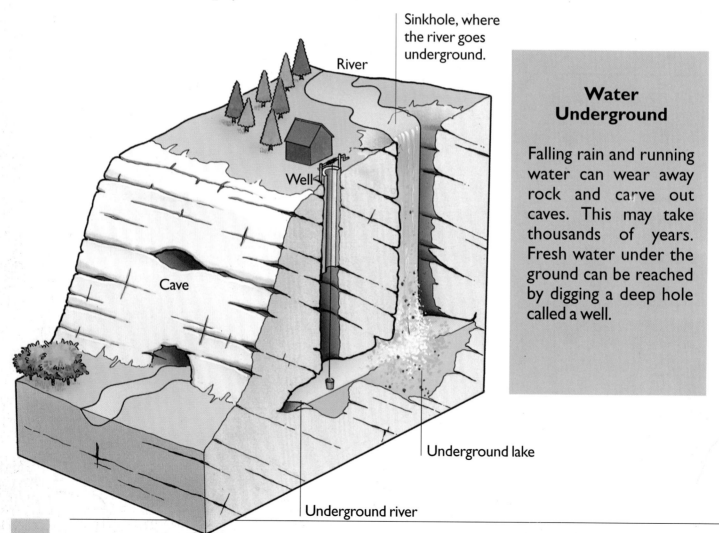

River

Sinkhole, where the river goes underground.

Well

Cave

Water Underground

Falling rain and running water can wear away rock and carve out caves. This may take thousands of years. Fresh water under the ground can be reached by digging a deep hole called a well.

Underground lake

Underground river

Children swim in a pool filled by a river. The pool is a hollow in the ground at the bottom of a waterfall. It is known as a splash pool.

19

Frozen Solid

Snow forms when water droplets in clouds freeze into specks of ice. As the specks float in the clouds, they join to make crystals. Then the crystals join to make snowflakes.

When the temperature is very low, water on the ground freezes. The water forms ice, which is solid and hard.

Near the North Pole, icebergs —blocks of ice bigger than some buildings—float in the cold waters of the Arctic Ocean.

In the wintertime in some places, snow that has fallen from clouds covers the landscape.

Water in Rivers

Snow and ice melt in warm sunlight. Melted water from snow-topped mountains rushes downhill into streams and rivers.

Rainwater collects in reservoirs and lakes. Lakes flow into rivers. Water for our homes is taken from reservoirs and rivers. But first the water is thoroughly cleaned.

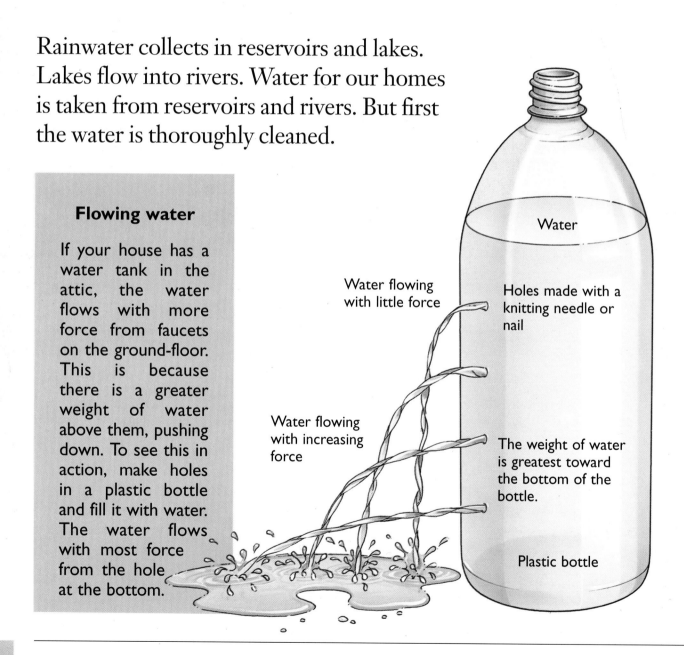

Flowing water

If your house has a water tank in the attic, the water flows with more force from faucets on the ground-floor. This is because there is a greater weight of water above them, pushing down. To see this in action, make holes in a plastic bottle and fill it with water. The water flows with most force from the hole at the bottom.

Water flowing with little force

Water flowing with increasing force

Water

Holes made with a knitting needle or nail

The weight of water is greatest toward the bottom of the bottle.

Plastic bottle

Streams contain fresh water, so-called because it is newly made from rain. Unlike seawater, it contains little or no salt.

At a water treatment plant, samples of water are taken regularly and tested to make sure the cleaning process is working properly.

Clean Water for All

River water must be cleaned before we drink it. Leaves, twigs, dead animals, plants, garbage, and sewage waste make river water dirty. Drinking it would make you sick.

River water is cleaned at a waterworks. Then it is pumped along big underground pipes called water mains. Small pipes take it from the mains to our homes.

At the waterworks

Fresh water from rivers is made suitable for us to drink or use in our homes at a waterworks. Some water companies add the chemical chlorine to fresh water to kill any germs. Often, they also add fluorine, a similar chemical that helps prevent tooth decay.

Water is stored, ready for use.

Water is collected behind a dam.

The filter beds trap sand, gravel, and dirt.

Mains to homes

Water from the dam flows into a reservoir.

A pumping station pours the water into filter beds.

25

THE WATER CYCLE

The water we drink has been around the world millions of times. Each drop from your faucet has been to a lake in Africa or an iceberg in the Arctic.

Drops of rain may fall on your roof, into the sea, or into the Zambezi River of Africa. Water moves from sky to land and land to sky, over and over again.

Water from Lake Victoria tumbles into the Zambezi River. The Zambezi flows into the Indian Ocean.

When heavy rain falls, a river can burst its banks and flood the surrounding countryside, as here in California.

Saving Water

Sometimes there is not enough water.
When it is dry, you can save water by not
watering the garden or washing the car.

Using Fresh Water

On the average, we
use about 53 gallons
(200 l) of water a day.
But we need only
about 21 gallons (80 l).
One way of cutting
down on the amount
of water you use is to
never leave faucets
running.

During a drought, when it
has not rained for several
weeks, it is best to water
plants with a watering can
instead of a hose.

To keep water clean and not block pipes, do not pour paints and oils into drains or allow candy wrappers and pieces of paper to fall into sewers. In that way, there will be clean water for the world's future generations.

Spring water—also known as mineral water—pouring into a glass filled with ice cubes. Spring water has little or no added chemicals like chlorine.

GLOSSARY

Boiler A heater that burns coal, oil, or gas or uses electricity to heat water in a building.

Chlorine A chemical added to water in swimming pools or at a waterworks to kill any germs.

Crystal A small solid shape with a regular pattern that some chemicals form when they change from liquid to solid form. Snowflakes, sugar, and salt are made of crystals.

Cycle A continuous round-and-round process.

Evaporation When liquid water is heated and becomes a gas called water vapor.

Filter Equipment that allows water to flow through but holds back sand, grit, and other solids.

Ice Frozen water, formed when the temperature of the water falls below 32° F (0° C).

Plant Usually, a living thing such as a flower or tree. The word "plant" can also mean a factory where goods are made or water is cleaned.

Pollution Poisonous dirt, chemicals, or artificial waste in air, soil, or water.

Reservoir An artificial lake where water is stored for use by people.

Sewage Waste from toilets, baths, and sinks.

Waste Garbage; anything that is left over or not wanted.

Water vapor Tiny drops of water in the air; steam or clouds, for example.

FURTHER READING

Costa-Pau, Rosa, et. al. *Protecting Our Rivers and Lakes* (Junior Library of Ecology). New York: Chelsea House, 1994.

Goldman, Linda. *Cleaning Up Our Water* (Restoring Nature: Success Stories). Danbury, CT: Children's Press, 1997.

Hoffman, Mary. *Earth, Fire, Water, Air.* New York: Dutton Children's Books, 1995.

Morgan, Sally and Adrian Morgan. *Water* (Design in Science). New York: Facts on File, 1994.

Oxlade, Chris. *Science Magic with Water* (Science Magic). Hauppauge, NY: Barron's, 1994.

Ward, Alan. *Water and Floating* (Project Science). Danbury, CT: Franklin Watts, 1992.

Wheeler, Jill C. *Every Drop Counts—A Book About Water.* Edina, MN: Abdo and Daughters, 1993.

Wick, Walter. *A Drop of Water: A Book of Science and Wonder.* New York: Scholastic Press, 1997.

INDEX